Burnham

Boy

Horatio Lord Nelson

*There have been many books about Horatio Nelson:
this booklet is not intended to compete.
It is the briefest look at the great man, with an
entirely local bias.*

Graham Pooley

JPB

©1990 Graham Pooley
Published by Jim Baldwin
Publishing Solutions
Fakenham NR21 8LQ
www.jimbooks.co.uk

Reprinted 1991
2nd Reprint 1994
3rd Reprint 1996
4th Reprint 1998
5th Reprint 1999
6th Reprint 2002
7th Reprint 2004
8th Reprint Trafalgar Bicentenary Year 2005
9th Reprint 2008
10th Reprint 2011

ISBN 978 0 9516120 0 2

Cover board and text paper FSC Certified Products.

Printed by L F Everett & Son and Taylor Printing
Bound by Dickens Print Trade Finishers

Introduction

A small boy's interest in Horatio Nelson began on a fairground in Plymouth. The biggest West country showman was pulling on to the pitch where the rides were to be put together.

The great steam engines, brasses shining, each drawing a train of huge trailers, were led into the ground by Lord Nelson. This magnificent steamer was the very last of the famous showman engines by Burrell of Thetford, Norfolk. The driver was pleased to tell the story.

Business had been so bad for Anderton and Rowlands, that they doubted if the old established business would survive. Burrell had made what was to be the last twelve Showman engines, and as was their custom, had chosen names for them. The Bristol operators risked what they had to buy the only unsold Burrell, and insisted on a change of name.

When England was in great danger, Lord Nelson saved his country. We believe that his name-sake will save us".

Over:
Horatio Vice-Admiral Lord Nelson aged 43 by John Hoppner RA. 1801

Burnham Boy

Horatio Nelson was born on the 29th September 1758, in the Parsonage of All Saints Church, Burnham Thorpe, Norfolk, where his father, the Reverend Edmund Nelson was Rector. The house was close to the Burn, 'Nelson's River', that rises a few miles away, in the parish of Syderstone. It makes its way through Leicester Square Farm to Southgate, where it is augmented by a powerful spring, and by a brook from Waterden. The pleasant stream runs through South Creake to the bridge at North Creake, where it turns, to flow through Burnham Thorpe, and to the sea at Burnham Overy.

This was a time of Hanoverian neglect of churches, the Georges showing little interest in Anglican buildings. Edmund's Church was in a bad state, the South Aisle in ruins. The fine condition in which it is to be seen today, is due to the efforts of the Rev. John Levien, and his successor John Lister Knight, who died in 1900. Restoration was completed in time for the Centenary of Trafalgar in 1905.

A shortage of clergy, with plurality as the normal order, meant that Edmund had the care of souls in the Burnham parishes of Norton, Sutton, and Ulph. The Church of Saint Margaret of Antioch at Norton, was in poor condition, whilst that of Saint Ethelbert at Sutton was to be abandoned, and amalgamated with All Saints at Ulph. He held the living at Burnham Thorpe from 1755, until his resignation, just before his death in 1802. His successor, Daniel Everard built a new Rectory, the house where Horatio was born was demolished, a coach house built on the site.

In 1749, Edmund Nelson married Catherine, daughter of Doctor Maurice Suckling. In this pretentious time, efforts were made to keep up with the County. The Sucklings were higher on the ladder than the Nelsons, one having married a sister of Robert Walpole of Houghton. Catherine's brothers were to be of value to her children; Maurice was a naval captain, whilst William had influence in Customs and Excise.

Three children died in infancy, eight survived to Catherine and Edmund; William, Maurice, Susannah, Horatio, Ann, Edmund Suckling, and Catherine. Their mother died on Boxing Day 1767, aged 42, and was buried in the Chancel at Burnham Thorpe.

One stands by the plaque marking Horatio's birthplace, with the impression that little can have changed, apart from the absence of the Parsonage, from the days when he played by the Burn, and later, cultivated his father's glebe. Winds blow as strongly as ever, across what he knew as the German Ocean.

Willian was destined for the Church, Maurice was found a post by his uncle, Horatio wanted the Navy. This was not easy; ships were laid up, officers on half pay. Captain Maurice Suckling was living quietly at

Woodton, Norfolk, when an adventure blew up in the Falklands, and offered employment. The Islands had been claimed by Britain in 1764, when the Union Flag was hoisted; in 1770, Spaniards lowered the Flag, and there was a stir of action at the Admiralty. Suckling was given a ship, enabling him to have Horatio entered as midshipman on the 1st January 1771, at the age of twelve.

The Royal Navy was able to use Nelson's talents fully for some years; lieutenant at eighteen, commander at twenty, and captain at twenty one. Linked as it was to war, promotion came to a halt; he held captain's rank for seventeen years. His frail father, finding Norfolk winters a trial, began to spend these months in Bath, where he apprenticed Susannah to a milliner. Edmund was a clerk for the Boltons of Wells, Norfolk, a family of corn and coal merchants, Suckling was apprenticed to a draper, whilst Anne died in 1784.

In that year, Horatio was appointed to command of the frigate Boreas, to take civilian passengers to the Caribbean, and remain there, looking after British business interests. It is doubtful if he was the right man for what proved to be an awkward assignment. He was a man of action, and may not have possessed the tact that would have eased this task. This was the aftermath of the American War, with Navigation Acts decreeing that American merchants trading with British colonies, were to be regarded as foreigners. The colonists had more sympathy with their American suppliers than with politicians who laid down unrealistic laws.

Nelson's efforts to carry out his instructions led to complaints of 'high handed actions by very young officers'. With what little social life there was at his base of Antigua increasingly denied to him, he found life dull until he met Mary Moutray. Always interested in women, Horatio found the young wife of the elderly Commandant to be very attractive, and was upset when they returned to England. The death of Moutray, soon after arriving home, causes Nelson's biographers to speculate on the difference there might have been if the Commandant had died in Antigua, leaving Nelson free to marry Mary Moutray.

Nelson was supported by John Herbert, the President of Nevis, one of the most attractive of the islands, who invited him to his home at Montpelier. Herbert's hostess was his neice, Frances Nisbet, a widow with a young son. Fanny, as she was known, the daughter of Judge William Woolward, had lived for most of her life on Nevis. Nelson's social life improved with the arrival in November 1786 of Prince William, son of George III, in command of the frigate Pegasus. The Prince, who was to make a tour of the islands, asked for the company of his old friend Captain Nelson. When Fanny and Horatio were married on the 11th March 1787, at Montpelier, the Prince was best man. Soon after they left for England, where Boreas was to be used to receive pressed men.

Nothing appears to have been recorded of Nelson's private opinion of the cruel practice of pressing civilians for service in the Navy, without concern for their families or circumstances. However, we know that he regarded merchant seamen as fair game, from an incident in October 1781. He was to escort convoys, with three ships, and found that they were all undermanned. He intercepted four merchantmen in the Thames, sailing together for added protection against this very hazard. The captains all ignored his signals to stop, until a broadside splashed around the leader. They had to submit to losing as many members of their crews as were needed by the naval vessels. No democrat, one wonders what Nelson thought of Samuel Johnson's opinion in one of his letters to Lord Chesterfield.

"No one will be a sailor, who has the contrivance to get into jail; being in a ship is being in jail with a chance of drowning. One in jail, has more room, better food, and better company".

When Boreas paid off in November 1787, Nelson discovered that reports from the Indies had given him the reputation of trouble maker, and compaints from the merchants had reached the King. His long wait for a ship had begun; he was 'on the beach' until 1793, when the situation was such, that every officer was called into service. The Rev. Edmund was delighted with his daughter-in-law, they were friends for the rest of his life. He rented a cottage in Ulph, so that they had the house to themselves, and took services in his favourite church, 'my chapel of ease'.

Captain Suckling died, leaving legacies; Susannah's enabled her to leave her employment and return to Norfolk, where she married Thomas Bolton of Wells. William had become a cleric, Maurice was at a desk in London, Suckling used his legacy to buy a shop in North Elmham, Edmund was 'in decline', Katherine had made a happy marriage to George Matcham. Horatio and Fanny settled into life in the Parsonage on half pay of eight shillings a day. Having lived in sunshine, Fanny found life in the Rectory in winter, hard to bear.

Farming the thirty acres of glebe, Horatio discovered that farm workers were in difficulties, and he wrote to Prince William of their attempts to keep a family on £23 a year. During these unblemished years he was received by T. W. Coke at Holkham, by Sir Mordaunt Martin at Burnham Polstead Hall, and, especially by the Rev. Doctor Charles Poyntz, the Rector of North Creake. In this nearby village, at the Old Parsonage, he met the Rector's family; his sister Countess Spencer and her daughters, Georgiana Duchess of Devonshire, and Harriet Countess Bessborough. Horatio's brother Edmund died; Suckling failed as a shopkeeper, and trained for the Church.

The Admiralty, failing to appreciate the significance to Britain of the storming of the Bastille on the 14th July 1789, continued to turn down Nelson's applications. Each Saturday he rode into Westgate for the Norfolk Chronicle, and the news from Revolutionary France. The call did not come until the 6th January 1793, when he was given command of Agamemnon. One of the Norfolk men who volunteered to join him was William Hoste, son of his father's friend, the Rector of Tittleshall. The French beheaded their King on the 25th January, and declared war on the 1st February. After a

Left: Nelson's letter, offering the sword of the Spanish Admiral to the city of Norwich.

Below: J S Cotman's drawing dated 1817, of Burnham Ulph Church, with St. Ethelbert's on the left.

farewell party at the Plough, in Thorpe, Nelson filled his ship with East Anglians. The long blockade of French ports began, during the course of which Nelson made the acquaintance of the British Minister to King Ferdinand of Naples, Sir William Hamilton, and his wife Lady Emma.

A base was needed for the Mediterranean fleet, so much of 1794 was taken up with a campaign to capture the island of Corsica. Naval landing parties fought their way towards Calvi, a town on the West coast. On the 12th July, a shell threw stones into Horatio's face, resulting in the loss of the sight of his right eye. He continued aboard, during the long campaign, until the island was taken.

In the following years, things went badly for Britain; the French recovered Corsica, and made such progress that the Admiralty ordered that the Mediterranean be evacuated. Morale was low, a victory was needed badly.

Fame came to Nelson in 1797, his day of glory was that of Saint Valentine, the 14th February. On the 13th, Nelson's lookout caught sight of an enemy fleet, and he reported to Sir John Jervis, his Commander-in-Chief. It proved to be a combined fleet of 27 French and Spanish ships. An action was fought in the waters of the great sweep of the Spanish Atlantic coast, northwards from Gibralter, that has gone into history as the Battle of Cape Saint Vincent. Jervis ordered his 15 ships into a line action against the larger enemy fleet.

Nelson saw a serious situation develop; realising that Jervis was not in a position to deal with it, he left his position in the line, and struck at the head of the enemy column, attacking seven Spaniards. Collingwood, Troubridge, and Frederick, joined Nelson, as with sails shot away, he rammed two Spaniards. Leading a boarding party, he captured the San Nicholas, and went on to take the San Josef. That evening he went aboard the flagship, expecting a reprimand for the sin of breaking line, but was thanked by Sir John, who had watched the operation with delight. Jervis was created Earl Saint Vincent; Nelson was promoted Rear Admiral. In May he was gazetted Knight of the Order of the Bath.

Horatio wrote to the Mayor of Norwich asking leave to present to the City, the sword of the Spanish Rear Admiral, who had died in the action. His offer was accepted, and he was made a freeman of Norwich. Our facsimile of his letter, dated 26th February 1797, is one of the last to have been written with his right hand. In April he sent drawings of the action to Fanny, writing, "My winter's gift to Burnham will be fifty blankets, to be at the disposal of my father".

A raid had been planned on ships from South America, at Teneriffe, and Sir Horatio made a will, leaving £200 to Maurice, £300 to his step-son, and the remainder to Fanny. Leading a landing party on the 25th July 1797, he was wounded in the right arm, and it was amputated, above the elbow. Saint Vincent sent him home with Captain Fremantle, cared for by Tom Allen, one of the Burnham Thorpe volunteers. He was invested by the King, and granted a pension of £900 per year for wounds and service.

The Government was given a forecast of what was to come, by Saint Vincent, one of our most far seeing Admirals. France would suspend plans to invade England, in favour of expansion in the East. He was shown to have been right, when a French fleet embarked an army, captured Malta, and went on to Alexandria, early in 1798. This army was led by General Napoleon Bonaparte, who landed unopposed at Marabout, won the Battle of the Pyramids, and became a threat to the Middle East, and to India.

The career of Rear Admiral Sir Horatio Nelson had been watched by Earl Spencer, first Lord of the Admiralty, who had made his acquaintance through the Rev. Doctor Poyntz. In April 1798, senior admirals were passed over, and Nelson was given command of the Mediterranean fleet, and a beat nearly two thousand miles in length. He heard that a fleet had left Toulon to bring back the victorious French army, and sailed for Alexandria. It was empty; the two fleets had missed one another. Nelson left the port and was barely out of sight when Admiral Brueys arrived with the Toulon fleet.

He was told that a fleet had sailed East on the 20th May, realised what had happened, returned to Egypt, and on the 1st August saw Brueys in Aboukir Bay, near to one of the outlets of the Nile. The French position was protected by shoals, and an island, upon which a battery had been mounted. It was late in the day, but Nelson decided to strike at once.

Brueys, who must have considered that his position was impregnable, chose to fight at anchor. It was his last engagement; the action went on throughout the night, and he directed, badly wounded, until he was killed. The Commodore of his flagship L'Orient was Casabianca, who had with him his ten years old son. The boy has been immortalised by Felicia Hemans, in her ballad beginning,

"The boy stood on the burning deck, whence all but he had fled",

and ending,

"but the noblest thing that perished there, was that young faithful heart".

Injured by a heavy blow to his forehead, Nelson was below when the L'Orient exploded; he returned in time to see its end. Dawn showed that fifteen enemy ships had sunk, or been taken, and that two had escaped. This remarkable night action wrecked Napoleon's plans for embarking his army, and might well be said to have changed world events. Bonaparte returned to France, leaving his army marooned, and established himself as dictator. Revolutionary France was now Napoleonic France. This was the beginning of the famous stalemate that has been called The Whale and the Elephant, with Britain in control of the sea, whilst Napoleon began to control most of Europe. Following his defeat of the Austrians at Marengo, and his occupation of Northern Italy, Napoleon succeeded in bluffing the British into accepting the Peace of Amiens. When he declared war again in May 1803, he had gained the time that he had played for. In November 1798, Sir Horatio was gazetted Baron Nelson of the Nile and Burnham Thorpe.

For friends of Nelson, a distressing period of his life began when he renewed his friendship with the Hamiltons, and became infatuated with Emma. Oliver Warner, a Hamilton biographer, wrote, "Sir William was 61 when he married Emma Lyon in 1791. She was 35 years younger, and Hamilton is reported to have said that in due course, 'he expected to be super-annuated'. The blow to Nelson's forehead had caused concussion and affected his sight. It has been suggested that it caused a personality change".

Nelson was nursed back to health in the Hamiltons' home in Palermo, then acted as deputy to Lord Keith, who had to go to England. He would not listen to friends who tried to persuade him that Palermo was not well placed to be his base. The King of Naples created him Duke of Brontë, and he assumed this title without having obtained the permission of his King.

In December he joined Lord Keith, and off Malta they captured one of the French ships to have escaped from Aboukir Bay. Once more Keith had to return to England, and he instructed Nelson to take command of the blockade of Malta. However, he left Sir Edward Berry in his place, and returned to Palermo. This sort of behaviour went on until Lord Spencer took a hand. In a carefully worded letter, he suggested to Nelson that he would not wish to remain inactive at a foreign court.

In July 1800, the Hamilton party set off for home overland, and reached Yarmouth in November, where Nelson was made a Freemen. The meeting of Fanny and Emma must have been awkward; Emma was pregnant and there was no attempt to suggest that Sir William was the father. The situation became known and diminished Nelson's achievements; the Press realised that Hamilton accepted the position, and he was caricatured. George III made it clear that he did not approve. Fanny found that her friends were the Rev. Edmund, and her brother-in-law Maurice. William Nelson, and Sarah his wife, attached themselves to the Hamiltons.

In 1801, a naval expedition was sent to Denmark, to persuade that country to allow the British fleet access to the Baltic Ocean. Condemned by many at the time as illegal, the action was due to concern about the possible activities of the Northern Coalition of Denmark, Norway, Sweden, Russia, and Prussia. During the American War, they had formed the Armed Neutrality of the North, to defend their rights to trade at sea, free of search. The British fleet was commanded by Sir Hyde Parker.

At this point, Nelson heard that Emma had given birth to a girl named Horatia. She had produced twins, and there are conflicting reports about the other baby. Fanny made the break, and her husband arranged to pay her an allowance. He sailed in the San Josef, the ship that he had captured four years earlier. In his journal, opened on the 13th March 1801, he described the Danish fleet, anchored in shallow water before Copenhagen, surrounded by blockships, and land forts.

The British anchored above Kronberg, where soundings revealed that there was not enough depth for the bigger ships. Admiral Parker stood off with these vessels, whilst Nelson transferred his flag to the Elephant, with

Captain Thomas Foley. His orders were to put the Danish fleet out of action, without harming the Captial. As the action progressed, Sir Hyde was not able to see anything except that two ships were aground, so he flew Signal 39, 'Discontinue Action'.

Much has been written about what followed; we give Thomas Foley's recollection. Elephant was flying Signal 16, 'Close Action'; Nelson said, "I have the right to be blind sometimes". Putting his telescope to his right eye, he said, "I really do not see the signal". Number 16 continued to fly until most of the Danish ships had been silenced, and their flagship exploded, when Nelson ceased fire. He sent a letter to their Prince Regent, who agreed that hostilities should cease. This was another action, after which Horatio went to the flagship expecting reprimand, but received praise for initiative.

He returned to Yarmouth, to be informed of the death at 47, of his favourite brother Maurice; he and William were the survivors of Catherine's eight sons. In August he was gazetted Viscount Nelson of the Nile and Hilborough, and obtained permission to adopt the title of Duke of Brontë, regularising its use. He was given command of the Channel Fleet, and commissioned to organise sea defence against an army known to be assembling on the shores of France. His work in Egypt had been continued

Nelson's birthplace, Burnham Thorpe, demolished 1802.

on land by Sir Ralph Abercrombie, and the Navy had taken Malta. Napoleon Bonaparte, needing time, managed in October 1801, the Peace of Amiens, to the despair of Nelson. However, it gave him a peaceful interlude; he bought Merton, a large house near Wimbledon, where he was joined by the Hamiltons. This lasted until May 1803, when war with France recommenced. Nelson's father died on the 26th April 1802, just before he was eighty, and a year later, Sir William Hamilton died.

Viscount Nelson was appointed Vice Admiral of the Blue, with command of the Mediterranean fleet, in flagship Victory, captained by Thomas Masterman Hardy. He now reached his highest rank, Vice Admiral of the White. In May 1804, off Ushant, he wrote, "Probably I shall not see dear Burnham again; I have the satisfaction of thinking that my bones will rest with my father's, in the village of my birth". Increasing fame must have raised the possibility in his mind of a national burial; for he was to say later that he desired to be buried in Saint Paul's.

Napoleon was declared Emperor of the French on the 14th March 1804, and his successes on land encouraged him to revive plans for the invasion of England. He knew that success would depend upon control of the Straits of Dover; the stupidity of the Peace of Amiens had given time to build up the French navy. Strangely, Bonaparte does not seem to have realised how much he had to gain by waiting, that time was on his side. Whilst constant blockading was wearing the strength of the British navy, twenty ships were well advanced in French yards, and the Spanish fleet was increasing.

Fortunately, Napoleon refused to endure the blockade; ships were held in Brest and Rochefort, whilst his Toulon fleet was prohibited from leaving port by Nelson. Admiral Latouche-Treville was ordered to break out, raise the blockade, and make for the Straits of Dover.

"Let us be masters of the Straits for six hours, and we shall be masters of the World".

The presence of Nelson inhibited Admiral Latouche-Treville, until he died of a heart attack. He was replaced by Admiral Pierre Villeneuve, perhaps the last man who should have been chosen. Having escaped with his ship from Aboukir Bay, he had a lasting fear of Nelson. The blockade continued until the 11th January 1805, when the Rochefort ships escaped during a snow-storm. Nelson remained outside Toulon, until spring gales made this position impossible.

In March he tempted Villeneuve by withdrawing to a position off Sardinia. The Frenchman was given high sounding intructions; 'leave port, conquer the West Indies, return around Scotland, and enter the Channel'. Bonaparte estimated that during this process, his Admiral would have built the strength of his fleet to 60 ships. As Nelson was not be be seen, Villeneuve made his break from Toulon, with 19 ships on the 30th March. He appeared off Cadiz, signalled to the ships there to join him, and disappeared. In London, where the danger to the West Indies was understood, and where there could be no news, there was great anxiety.

Nelson went to the Indies in vain; Villeneuve had been, heard that the man he feared was near, abandoned his orders, and sailed for Europe. Horatio made a rapid run to Gibraltar, where he set foot ashore for the first time in two years. His popularity began to return when news of removal of the threat to the Indies became known. Damage to his standing, caused by his affair with Emma, and by his desertion of his wife, was beginning to be overlooked. He returned to Portsmouth on the 18th August 1805, and was joined by his family at Merton.

The French army was gathered at Channel ports, awaiting ships to take it to England. Having collected various parts of the scattered fleet, Villeneuve made for Corunna, and by being so far South, ruined the invasion plan. His fleet of 25 French and Spanish ships was seen by Cuthbert Collingwood, who sent Captain Henry Blackwood home with the news. Blackwood called at Merton, and Nelson went to London, where Lord Barham, now First Lord, asked him to assume command.

Horatio said, "At this time of the year, the day is not long enough to arrange a fleet in order of sail, and then have time for a decisive battle. When we meet, we shall fight according to a plan that I shall give my captains". He left Portsmouth for the last time, on 1st September 1805.

On the 29th, his 47th birthday, fifteen captains came aboard Victory, and were given his plan of attack. It is not possible for us to know what magic those men experienced in his presence. Few had been under his command, or had taken a big ship into battle. All were prepared to believe that he had inherited 'The Admiral's Mirror', and they followed him in full confidence. Spaniards of the time of Sir Francis Drake had talked of an enchanted looking glass, in which the English Admiral saw their movements.

The attack was to be in two lines; Lee Division led by Cuthbert's Royal Sovereign, and Weather Division led by Nelson in Victory. News reached Villeneuve that he was to be replaced, and this spurred him into leaving harbour. At 6 am on Saturday the 19th October 1805, a frigate made the signal, 'Enemy topsails hoisted'. The British made for Gibraltar, sighting the enemy off Cadiz on Sunday evening. Nelson headed in the same direction as that taken by Villeneuve, and by dawn on Monday was in the position he had aimed for, nine miles to windward, and heading in the direction of Gibraltar.

At 6.30 am, 'Prepare for Action' was signalled. Villeneuve gave the order to form line of battle, by now close to the shoals off Cape Trafalgar. The British approached with the advantage of the wind, in the planned two lines.

Nelson made his last entry in his diary, 11am Monday 21st October 1805, noting that it was the day of Burnham Thorpe Fair. Collingwood's Lee Division cut into Villeneuve's single line at an angle, about fifteen ships from its rear. Victory, Neptune, and Temeraire of Weather Division attacked the enemy van. The wheel of Victory was destroyed; steered by tiller from the lower deck, it closed Villeneuve's flagship, and there was close fighting all along the line for several hours. At 1.15pm Hardy saw Nelson was on the deck.

Lewis Rotely was a young Marine officer who had met Nelson when he was a boy. He described what happened. "I saw the mizzen of Redoubtable crowded with marines, firing at a particular part of the deck of Victory. My men vollied into them but we were too late to prevent the fatal shot, and I saw Lord Nelson fall".

Horatio was carried below, attended by Sir William Beatty, whose account states that a musket ball entered his chest and lodged in his spine. At 2.30pm, Hardy brought the news that 12 enemy ships had surrendered... Beatty went on, "They have done for me Hardy, don't throw me overboard. Take care of my dear Lady Hamilton". He died at 4.30pm. The enemy had been overcome, Villeneuve was a prisoner, no British ship had been lost.

Lewis Rotely made a point of seeing the place where his hero had died, and found in a corner the bloodstained breeches and stockings. He asked for them, and strangely, was allowed to take them. These items were in his family until they were presented to the National Maritime Museum.

In a rising gale, the fleet was in danger of running on to the Trafalgar shoals; many of the captured ships had to be abandoned, only four were brought into Gibraltar. Victory reached the Rock with Nelson in a cask of rum, had emergency repairs, and limped to Spithead by the 4th December. The Admiral lay in state in the Painted Hall, Greenwich until the 8th January 1806. The funeral procession, on the 9th, was from the Admiralty to Saint Paul's. The official Chief Mourner was the 85 year old Admiral of the Fleet, Sir Peter Parker, under whom Horatio had served as Third Lieutenant, and who had promoted him to First Lieutenant.

From many accounts of the last moments of Nelson, we select that of the Times, whose correspondent was aboard Victory. Its entire issue of the 7th November was devoted to descriptions of the Battle of Trafalgar, with lists of casualties, and a poem in his honour. Its account of the sea fight was by Vice Admiral Cuthbert Collingwood, who lies in the Crypt of Saint Paul's, a few paces to the left of his friend.

The Times man wrote that Nelson was wounded by a ball that went into his chest, and surgeons saw no hope, Captain Hardy came to tell of the ships that had struck colours. Nelson gave some warning of the impending gale and said, "I am dying; I wish that I could have breathed my last upon British ground, but the will of God be done". In a few moments, he expired.

An effect of the victory of Trafalgar that is rarely mentioned, was the problem of dealing with large numbers of captured Frenchmen and Spaniards. The Napoleonic Wars continued to be fought on land for another ten years, and most of the unfortunate prisoners were held until after the defeat of France at Waterloo. Old naval vessels were used as prison hulks whilst prisons were built on Dartmoor, and at Norman Cross, Huntingdonshire. A letter found in a trinket made by one reads "Joseph Dedoue made this box in 1814. Taken at Waterloo, these scoundrels have held me for nearly ten years, in their prison at Norman Cross. 26 April 1814".

The Reverend Doctor William Nelson, Horatio's only surviving brother, without effort, acquired a higher rank in the Peerage. Parliament had arranged, before Trafalgar, that Nelson's Barony, but not his Viscounty, would be remaindered to his father, his father's sons, nephews, and neices. After the great victory, it was thought that a Barony was not sufficient commemoration. The Rev. Williams was created First Earl Nelson, his only son becoming Viscount Merton. This son, Horace, died in January 1808, aged 20, and was buried in the vault of Saint Paul's.

The Annual Register for 1808 stated, "By this death, the honours and estate of Lord Nelson will pass, on the death of the present Earl, from the male to the female line , through Mrs Susannah Bolton, sister of the gallant conqueror, whose son Thomas is the next in the remainder".

The Nelson Earldom carried a pension of £5,000 per year, for ever. 150 years later, this pension was taken away by the Government of the day. Horatio's surviving sisters, Susannah and Catherine, were granted £15,000 each, from the Nation. Fanny received a pension of £2,000 a year until her death in 1831. The Reverend William, seeing that the Earldom would leave his line, was able to arrange that the Dukedom of Bronte would descend in the female line, so that his only daughter Charlotte would benefit.

Charlotte Nelson married the Hon. Samuel Hood, later Baron Bridport, and on the death of her father inherited the Dukedom of Bronte. Eventually the Bridport family sold the estate to the town authority.

Emma took her daughter Horatia to Calais, and died there on the 15th January 1815. The Matchams rescued Horatia, and she made her home with this family. In 1822 she married the Rev. Philip Ward, the Curate of Burnham Westgate. The story of this happy marriage, together with that of Nelson's sisters, is one to be told on another occasion.

Footnote: The Curate of Haworth, whose name was Brunty, changed it to Brontë. His daughters Anne, Charlotte, and Emily added their literary fame to the Nelson title.